HOW THEY
LIVED

AN AUSTRALIAN
PIONEER

NIGEL HUNTER

Illustrated by
Mark Bergin

HOW THEY LIVED

An American Pioneer Family
An Australian Pioneer
An Aztec Warrior
A Celtic Family
A Child in Victorian London
A Colonial American Merchant
A Crusading Knight
An Edwardian Household
A Family in the Fifties
A Family in World War I
A Family in World War II
An Ice Age Hunter
An Inca Farmer
A Medieval Monk
A Medieval Serf
A Norman Baron

A Plains Indian Warrior
A Plantation Slave
A Roman Centurion
A Roman Gladiator
A Sailor with Captain Cook
A Samurai Warrior
A Saxon Farmer
A Schoolchild in World War II
A Slave in Ancient Greece
A Soldier in Wellington's Army
A Soldier in World War I
A Teenager in the Sixties
A Tudor Merchant
A Victorian Factory Worker
A Viking Sailor

Editor: Amanda Earl

First published in 1987 by
Wayland (Publishers) Limited
61 Western Road, Hove
East Sussex BN3 1JD, England

All words that appear in **bold**
in the text are explained
in the glossary on page 31.

British Library Cataloguing in Publication Data
Hunter, Nigel
An Australian pioneer. – (How they lived).
1. Frontier and pioneer life – Australia
– Juvenile literature 2. Australia
– Social life and customs – Juvenile literature
I. Title   II. Series 994.02   DU115

ISBN 1 85210 199 7

Typeset by Kalligraphics Limited, Redhill, Surrey
Printed and bound in Belgium by Casterman S.A.

CONTENTS

TRANSPORTED

Tom was feeling utterly miserable. Of all the cruel fates he could imagine, this was surely the worst. To be **transported** to an unexplored land on the far side of the world – just another convict among a whole company of scoundrels! He was aboard the first fleet, bound for New South Wales.

At least Tom still had a future. In 1787, he could have been sentenced to death for stealing a pocket handkerchief. He was only fourteen, but children as young as eight sometimes faced the hangman. Instead, he would serve seven years helping to build the British Government's new prison **colony**, about 20,000km away. It was a hazardous venture, and nobody knew what to expect.

The voyage took eight months. There were eleven ships, carrying nearly 1,500 people. Just over half were convicts; the rest were Royal Marines, merchant seamen and men of the Royal Navy. Some Marines brought their families, and a few women convicts had young children too. The women were supposed to be kept separate from the male convicts and sailors, but this order was not always strictly obeyed.

Life below decks was cramped and unhealthy. Tom's bunk was only 40cm wide, and he shared it with all kinds of **vermin**. Foul-smelling **bilge water** swirled about the deck, and in storms the sea sometimes swept in and soaked him. The food was of poor quality and unvaried – mainly salted meat, bread, oatmeal, peas, vinegar and cheese. Marines patrolled among the prisoners all the time, and discipline was very strict. However, only the most troublesome convicts were locked in **irons**. The others were allowed on deck in fine weather. But the trip was long and uncomfortable, and nobody enjoyed it.

This book looks at life during the first decades of Australian **colonization** from 1788 to 1840, and describes the hardship and struggle that the early **pioneers** faced.

Conditions for convicts on the eleven ships bound for New South Wales were cramped and squalid.

4

THE 'UNKNOWN SOUTHLAND'

The Aborigines were the original Australian settlers, having lived there for many thousands of years before the Europeans arrived. Since ancient times, many Europeans had believed in the existence of a great southern landmass, in seas as yet unsailed. Some said that it simply had to be there, to 'balance' the northern continents. Otherwise, they claimed, the world would be top-heavy, and unable to turn properly.

The first Europeans to search seriously for the 'unknown Southland' (*Terra Australis Incognita*) were the Spanish. Sailing westward from

To the Aborigines who had lived in Australia for thousands of years, the sight of the first fleet was bewildering.

Peru, one attempt in 1606 came very close to success. The Torres Straits, off Australia's north-eastern tip, were named after this expedition's commander.

The first Europeans to actually land in Australia were the Dutch. Exploring to the south-east of their colonies in the East Indies, Willem Jansz discovered a barren, unwelcoming shoreline at a point he called Cape Turn-again.

Over the next forty years, Dutch voyagers managed to chart much of Australia's coast – often finding certain parts by total accident. But there seemed nothing of any value on the land, and the inhabitants appeared very poor people.

The British and French were the next to explore Australia, yet it took more than a century for anyone to find the eastern coast. When Captain James Cook succeeded, in 1770, the continent's outline became much clearer. Soon it was decided that this country would make an ideal convict colony.

HARD LABOUR

The first fleet landed at Botany Bay in January 1788, but as the harbour was poor here, they immediately moved two miles north to Sydney Cove, Port Jackson. At Port Jackson, (present day Sydney), the convicts' first big task was to clear the land and erect government and public buildings. Among these were a hospital, quayside and central storehouse. As the colony grew, the men were set to work in government workshops and offices; in flourmills and brickyards; and on government farms.

Some convicts were put into a **chain-gang**, and made to quarry stone or build roads. Their guards were often very brutal, and severe floggings for minor offences were

common. Convicts who carried on their lives of crime would be sent to more severe places of punishment, like Norfolk Island which was about 1,600km across the sea. Here, some men played terrible suicide games, drawing straws to choose a 'murderer' and 'victim'. They welcomed death as a release from their terrible life.

For most convicts life was not so desperate. Many became 'servants', working for individual settlers. They were not paid, but at least they had enough food and clothing. They also had some time during the day to themselves.

Among the population, male

Above *Badly behaved convicts were made to form a chain-gang, which was closely guarded by Marines.*

convicts outnumbered women several times over. The women convicts who had not become servants lived at Parramatta, 25km inland from the main settlement of Port Jackson. The 'factory', as it was called, was a dingy place where the women were made to sew and spin. Some convicts treated the factory as a 'marriage market', hoping to find a good wife!

Below *A view of Port Jackson and Sydney Cove in 1793 during the early years of the convict settlement.*

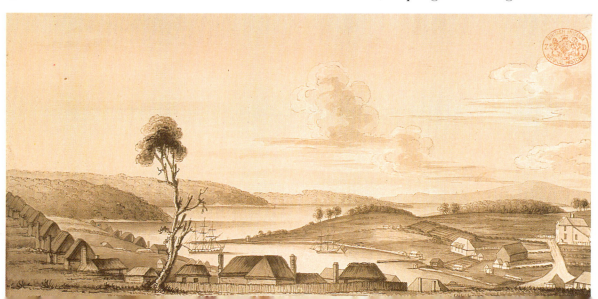

PARRAMATTA

A young convict such as Tom might eventually find himself working for the government at Parramatta. This was the first area to be settled after

A map showing the sites and dates of the earliest settlements in New South Wales and Tasmania. The state of Victoria, which would later include Melbourne, was not established until 1851.

Port Jackson. It was two days' journey up the Hawkesbury River, or half that time by road. The soil was more **fertile** at Parramatta. The government farm there consisted of about 80 hectares which was divided into areas for cattle farming and crop growing.

Most of the convicts lived in single-storey, two-roomed houses, each house being shared by ten or twelve men. The buildings were quite small, only about 8 by 3m, so conditions were very cramped. They had a basic wooden framework, with walls of **wattle** and clay, and a thatched roof. One room contained a fire-place and a brick chimney.

Convict **rations** were barely enough to keep them going – sometimes just a weekly issue of uncooked meat, **corn meal**, and wheat that had to be ground into flour, or a few potatoes and other vegetables; sometimes sugar and salt; sometimes tea and tobacco. Women convicts received only half the men's ration, and transported boys, only a quarter! At Parramatta some women lived in

communal huts, like the men. Among them were women whose job it was to keep the men's huts clean, and prepare the food.

Marriage was generally encouraged by the authorities. Married convicts could set up their own small-holding, where they could keep a few farmyard animals and a vegetable patch. While a single

Above *The Governor's house (centre) at Parramatta, surrounded by the convicts' houses. Notice the stocks to the right. Badly behaved convicts would have been locked in these for punishment.*

ex-convict was granted 12 hectares of land to **cultivate**, married ex-convicts could get nearly double that area.

Below *Accommodation was very basic. Up to twelve men shared a two-roomed house.*

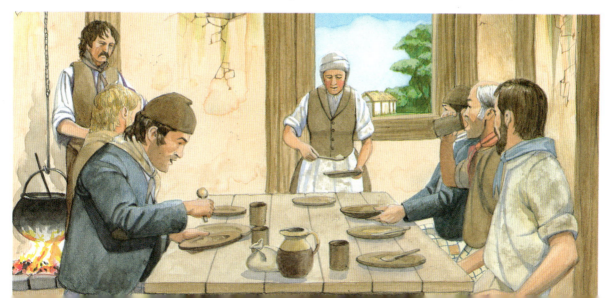

SET FREE

A convict coming to the end of his sentence would start considering his future. He might think about returning to Britain. But that cost money; and for the poor at home, as he would know from the stories the newly-transported prisoners told, conditions were not improving. He might consider finding employment as a free man, doing the same sort of work as the convicts did, but being paid for it. Or he might decide to take up a **land-grant**.

Convicts with experience of farm work knew of the difficulties and opportunities involved. The best farming area was a region about 50km to the north of Sydney, along the Hawkesbury River. By the mid 1790s there were about 400 settlers there, nearly ten per cent of the total population.

Married ex-convicts could expect a grant of 20 hectares (with an extra 4 hectares for every child). They had

The best farming land in New South Wales was alongside rivers like the Hawkesbury and Hunter. Freed convicts, like the men on the right, were allowed to set up farms in these areas.

This picture shows some early settlers on the outset of their journey from Melbourne. Ex-convicts often took up the government's offer of a land-grant. They would collect their supply of provisions, seeds and livestock and set off to establish a farm of their own.

to agree to work the land for at least five years. During that time, it was free, but then they would pay a shilling 'quit rent' per year for each 20 hectares. To start them off they would be given tools and seed from the government store, plus a small assortment of livestock. For the first year or two, the government would provide their food and clothing. They would also be entitled to one convict labourer!

Life for these settlers could be very lonely; they would have been glad of a partner to share the burdens.

THE HOMESTEAD

Ex-convicts were not the only pioneers. Free **migrants** were also starting to arrive in the colony, probably attracted by the generous land-grants they too could receive from the government. A single man was **eligible** for a grant of 52 hectares. Marines who had finished their service were entitled to the same amount; while retired officers, and an increasing number of serving officers as well, received 80 hectares or more. Some employed large numbers of convict labourers on their land, and became extremely

A typical homestead of a poor pioneer. There was always work to be done tending to the crops and livestock.

wealthy from the profit that the crops provided.

The better-off pioneers lived in houses of brick or stone, with roofs made of shingles (thin strips of timber arranged like tiles). Verandahs that stretched right around the house became very fashionable. In the townships, a few two-storey houses were beginning to be built. Some were very ornate and grand.

The poorer pioneers had to be content with simpler houses. For tools, they might have only a spade, a shovel, two hatchets and two hoes. Clearing a space amid the hardwood trees usually took a great deal of time and effort. But the trees provided good timber, which was used as the hut's corner-posts and door frames. The walls were made of a network of wattles, with mud packed in between which were then whitewashed. Thatched reeds made the roof, and packed mud the floor. There were usually two rooms and two windows, one room with a rough stone fireplace.

Above *Arthur Philip, the captain of the first fleet, became Governor of New South Wales. His house at Port Jackson, pictured above, was very grand and comfortable, unlike the simple pioneer homestead.*

Below *Typical examples of officers' homes at Parramatta.*

FOOD, DRINK AND PROVISIONS

Government provisions and land-grants were not given just out of generosity. The colony encouraged farming to maintain and increase its food supply. Pioneers were expected eventually to become self-supporting, and to sell any leftover food and produce to the public store. They also employed ex-convicts as farm-hands, which relieved the government of having to provide for them.

Until they were properly established on their farms, the poorer pioneers' diet would depend largely on what they were issued from the government stock. This was probably quite similar to what was supplied to convicts. The amount

A pioneer's home had little furniture, and food was cooked on an open fire.

provided might have been greater, its quality better, and 'luxury items' like sugar and vegetables less rare. But there was little variety, and mealtimes cannot have been much to look forward to.

Cooking utensils consisted of a couple of knives, an iron pot and a ladle. The pioneers would probably

Left *Settlers sometimes wove their own clothes from the flax plant.*

have eaten from wooden bowls and plates, with wooden spoons. Their furnishings would be simple, sparse and functional: tables and chairs of timber and beds of branches or saplings. Woollen blankets were considered quite a luxury.

Clothes would be made from materials close to hand. The flax plant was turned into linen cloth by soaking the stems in water, then beating

In Australia's hot, dry climate, there was a constant danger of water shortage. Pioneers often distilled fresh water from sea water, as this picture shows.

them into a stringy mass which could be spun into thread, and woven. The cloth was used to make smocks, shirts, trousers and skirts. Many farmers wore hats of plaited straw or caps made from kangaroo hide.

17

AGAINST THE ELEMENTS

In time, the pioneers' produce included grain (wheat, barley, maize and oats); meat (pork, mutton, beef and poultry); vegetables such as potatoes, turnips, beans and pumpkins; fruit such as oranges, peaches, lemons and grapes; plus cheese, butter and milk from cows or goats. But a farmer had to work very hard to be successful.

Much of the colony often suffered severe droughts. The temperature could rise to 40°C or higher. Rivers dried up, crops failed and livestock died. Near Parramatta one year, pioneers spoke of bats and even tropical birds dropping dead from the trees, 'unable to endure the burning state of the atmosphere longer'.

In the region of the Hawkesbury River, however, the main problem was flooding. Normally the river benefited the farmer. It enriched the land, and made it possible to produce twice as much wheat per hectare compared to elsewhere.

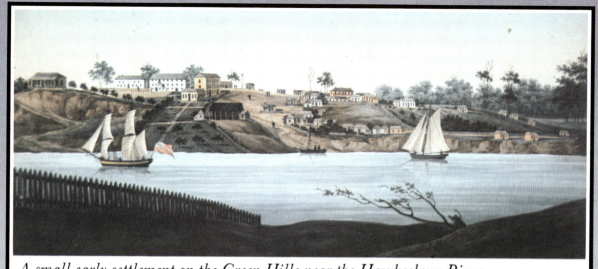

A small early settlement on the Green Hills near the Hawkesbury River.

But, the floods caused chaos. Around the turn of the eighteenth century there were major floods every few years. During one terrible eight-month period, the land was flooded four times. Crops were destroyed, and animals swept away and drowned. Occasionally people died as well. Others sometimes waited on rooftops for days to be rescued. Not surprisingly, many pioneers decided to leave this area for good.

Pioneers faced many problems when they set up their farms. The land around the Hawkesbury River flooded frequently.

THE RUM CORPS

Natural disasters, like droughts and floods, were not the only problems facing the poorer pioneers. The way in which the colony was run also caused problems.

For more than ten years, trading was controlled by officers of the New South Wales Corps. Between them, they owned almost all of the larger farming properties, which were worked by unpaid convict labour. They also controlled what was bought for the government store. They favoured the produce grown by fellow officers, paying the small farmers

In the early years in Australia, there was a shortage of currency. Goods, supplied from merchant ships (like the one below), acted as a form of currency.

low prices or, when harvests were good, not buying from them at all.

There was a general lack of currency in the colony. Goods were often bartered (exchanged) rather than bought and sold; and many people accepted goods rather than money as payment for work. But there was also another medium of exchange – **'rum'**, an alcoholic spirit usually made from wheat. Officers controlled most of the rum supplies. They purchased it from visiting merchant ships, or it was made in the officers' own illegal **stills**. They sold the rum at vast profits and were given the nickname 'the Rum Corps'.

Many of the poorer pioneers became addicted to rum, some exchanging a whole year's crops for just a few litres. The habit of drinking rum interfered with their work and many pioneers sunk into debt.

Right *For a time, the Rum Corps controlled whose farming produce was bought by the government. They would favour their friends' crops, turning away the crops of other poor pioneers.*

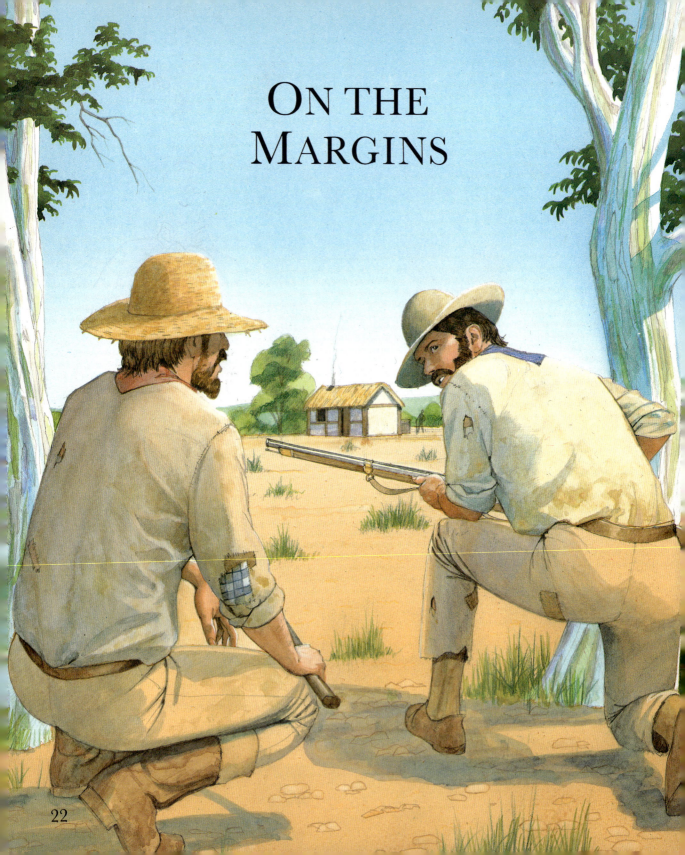

ON THE MARGINS

Small farmers on the edges of the settlement had to face other problems. Beyond their land was the wilderness known as the 'bush'. For anyone but the Aborigines, survival there was almost impossible. Escaped convicts who disappeared into the bush sometimes became so desperate that they gave themselves up, despite the harsh punishment they could expect. Yet, some of those who escaped did survive, and were known as 'bushrangers'.

They roamed the outskirts of the settlements, robbing travellers and stealing from the outlying farms. Some had friends among serving convicts and former convicts in the area, who provided them with food and information. Their raids became so frequent in one part of the colony that pioneers even **reinforced** the walls of their houses.

The Europeans forced many Aborigines to leave the land they had lived on for thousands of years. The *Cadigal* tribe were driven from the area around the Hawkesbury River into the Australian interior. The

On the arrival of the British in Australia, the Aborigines were forced into the interior of the country.

Europeans then cut down all the trees and even built houses on sacred sites that the Aborigines had worshipped for centuries. Aborigines did not understand the European idea of 'property'. Their land was given to them by the 'Ancestral Beings' – it could not be bought, sold or bartered.

The Aborigines wanted the Europeans to leave their country, and occasionally small groups of Aborigines would come out from the bush and try to take the livestock or crops of an isolated settler. Such settlers were issued with guns to protect what they now felt was 'their' land. In such confrontations, many Aborigines and pioneers were killed.

Left *Some convicts escaped into the bush, but it was hard to survive. They attacked small farms to get food and water.*

23

CHURCH AND SCHOOL

In the early life of the colony, religion and education had only a small part to play. But gradually both churches and schools began to appear.

The first church was built in Sydney in the mid-1790s by convicts who were paid by the minister partly in rum! Shortly after it was built, it

This is Windsor Church, near Sydney, built in the 1820s.

was burnt to the ground by convicts who resented having to attend religious services every week. The same minister also began the first three schools in the colony. Their main purpose was to teach the Christian gospel. But they were small and poorly attended, and like many others that followed, lasted for only a short time.

A school for orphan girls was also started which combined religious instruction with teaching in skills such as cooking, sewing and cleaning. This was to make the pupils acceptable as servants for the colony's wealthier pioneers. There was also a school run by the army for the children of serving soldiers. But for a long time, many pioneers' children received virtually no real education.

Ministers were given the task of teaching the children of poor pioneers.

A cross-section of society lived in Australia, but wealthier pioneers did not really mix with the poorer people.

In the early 1800s, however, parents in the Hawkesbury region paid for a combined schoolhouse and church to be built. The clergyman appointed to the church was also the children's teacher. Few of the district's 400 or so children attended regularly. They were needed at home most of the time to help with the farm work. But many probably attended often enough to learn to read and write, and do simple arithmetic.

25

PASTIMES

The poorer pioneers had little time or opportunity for entertainment. Most of their daylight hours were spent working hard on their land. During the evenings, in their candle-lit huts, many probably amused themselves with local gossip or by telling stories of former times, and their future hopes and dreams. Riddles, card-games and singing were other pastimes, and children invented various games and amusements to occupy themselves in the long winter evenings.

It was only in the townships that other sorts of activities existed. But by 1820, small towns had appeared in most of the settled areas. In the Hawkesbury region, several new towns were built on high ground, away from the ever-present threat of flooding. Each had a church and a school. For farming families, church

From the early days of Australian settlement, cricket was a popular pastime. This painting depicts a match at the 'Hyde Park' ground in the early 1820s. Behind the cricket green some interesting buildings can be seen – 1. The Supreme Court; 2. St. James Church; 3. Sydney Hospital; 4. Convict barracks.

Once the townships had become established, the social life of the rich pioneers and army officers flourished. Gala dinners and magnificent balls were very fashionable.

Dogfighting, cockfighting and boxing were popular entertainments, especially with those who liked to gamble. Drinking was also a common pastime, as, for many convicts, was brawling and thieving. Sometimes people gathered to watch the Aborigines' ritual meeting, known as a *'corroboree'*, that occasionally took place at night on the edge of town. Others found a more gruesome form of entertainment, from time to time, at public floggings and executions.

Boxing became a popular sport with some pioneers, especially if they gambled on the winner!

activities on Sundays became the most regular social event.

Sydney was the centre of colonial society. But ordinary farming folk living 50 or 60km away rarely visited the town. The most exciting events there were the races, held each year, which involved a whole week of entertainments, including grand balls and gala dinners. But these occasions were only for wealthy people.

EXPANSION

The Australian settlement that began as a simple 'dumping-ground' for British villains later became much more. By the late 1820s – nearly forty years after the first convicts arrived – New South Wales had a population of farmers and businesspeople, tradespeople, soldiers and civil servants, old people, young people, rich and poor. The settlement was also beginning to expand around the coast, and into the interior.

Norfolk Island's first pioneers landed in 1788, while Tasmania (then called Van Diemen's Land) was not established until 1803. Both were places of punishment for the most hardened criminals – but also developed farming and settlements in much the same way as on the mainland. To the north of Sydney

By the 1830s, some pioneers decided to venture into Australia's interior, particularly the rich pastures over the Blue Mountains, for this land was ideal for sheep farming.

was Moreton Bay (now called Brisbane). This began as an isolated penal settlement in 1825, but became open to free pioneers in the 1830s.

Elsewhere around the coast many adventurous people were making their mark. Sometimes they started out as small, independent groups; sometimes they had official government backing. Their struggles were such that many, particularly in Western Australia, gave up in despair. But others managed to establish themselves, and eventually prospered. The cities of Melbourne, Adelaide, Albany, Fremantle and Perth now occupy the sites where these pioneers first established their camps.

Tasmania, settled in 1803, soon developed into a farming community.

But it was the crossing of the great geographical barrier of the Blue Mountains in New South Wales that did most to speed up the pace of development. It opened the way to rich pastures for vast flocks of sheep. Before long, wool became Australia's main source of wealth.

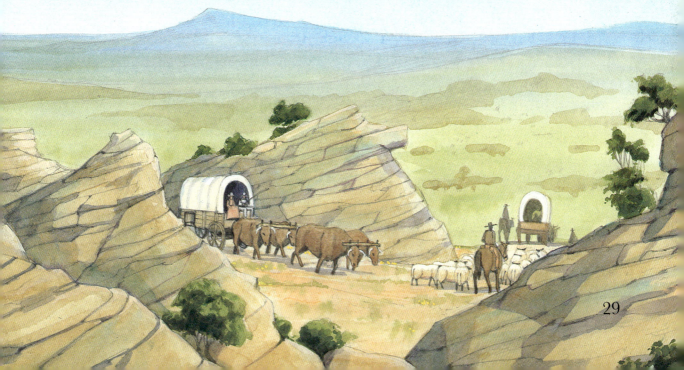

29

NEW FRONTIERS

The men and women who took their sheep and cattle over the mountains into the interior belonged to a new generation of pioneers. The era of transportation was gradually ending. There were various reasons for this. One reason was that people in Britain began to question such a brutal system of punishment.

Among the new pioneers were many free immigrants who chose to come to the colony, and an increasing number of people who were born there. Many were looking to the future, when Australia might become a self-governing nation; but before that, it had to cease being a penal settlement. Transportation to New South Wales eventually finished in 1840. It was the beginning of the end of the system.

Yet, nobody who lived through those hard early days of Australia's history would forget them.

This famous painting by Ford Madox Brown, called 'The Last of England', shows a couple who are immigrating to Australia in the 1850s. During this period many thousands of people saw Australia as a chance for a new start in life.

30

GLOSSARY

Bilge water   Dirty, stagnant water that collects in a ship's bilge (lower hull).

Chain-gang   A number of convicts chained together usually while carrying out heavy manual labour.

Colonization   The settling in a foreign land by immigrants from another country, forming a new community.

Colony   A foreign settlement governed by the settlers' country of origin.

Communal   Used or shared in common with a number of people.

Corn meal   A meal made from maize.

Cultivate   To work over and prepare a piece of land for planting and growing crops.

Eligible   To qualify for something.

Fertile   Fruitful; able to bear crops.

Irons   Heavy leg or wrist chains which make a prisoner's escape more difficult.

Land-grant   Gift or allowance of land.

Migrant   Someone who moves from one place to live in another.

Pioneer   A settler of a newly discovered land.

Ration   A strictly controlled allowance of food, clothing etc.

Reinforced   Strengthened by adding extra layers.

'Rum'   The term 'rum' described almost any alcoholic spirit. At this time, 'rum' was mainly made from wheat, not from molasses as today.

Still   A special apparatus used to produce alcoholic spirits such as rum, or whisky.

Transported   Sent to a prison colony.

Vermin   Small animals such as insects and rodents which spread disease.

Wattle   Twigs and branches which have been woven together to form a network, which is then plastered with clay or mud to make walls and fences.

MORE BOOKS TO READ

Adams, K. M. *The First Australians* (Angus and Robertson, 1969)

Adams, K. M. *Australia: Gaol to Colony* (Angus and Robertson, 1968)

Roderick, C. *Australia – History and Horizons* (Weidenfeld and Nicolson, 1971)

William, J. *The Exiles* (Shakespeare Head Press / Frederick Muller, 1972)

Unstead, R. J. and Henderson, W. F. *Pioneer Home Life in Australia* (A & C Black, 1971)

INDEX

Picture acknowledgements

The pictures in this book were supplied by the following: Aldus Archives 12, 17; Axel Poignant Archives 9 (bottom), 13, 15 (top), 20, 26, 27; BBC Hulton Picture Library 11 (top), 16 (right); The Bridgeman Art Library (Birmingham Museum and Art Gallery) 30; ET Archives 15 (bottom), 19, 24; The Mansell Collection 9 (top); Mary Evans Picture Library 29; Peter Newark's Western Americana 25. The remaining pictures are from Wayland Picture Library.